Animals and Nature

Text: Janine Amos, Andrew Solway
Consultant: Michael Chinery, M.A. & Dip. Anthropology (Cantab.)
Computer illustrations: Mel Pickering
Watercolor illustrations: Lindy Norton
Photo research: Jackum Brown and Vicki Walters

Editorial Director: Sue Hook
Art Director: Belinda Webster
Production Director: Lorraine Estelle
Editor: Lucy Duke
Assistant Editor: Deborah Kespert
Co-editions Editor: Robert Sved
Assistant Designers: Beth Aves, Helen McDonagh, Lisa Nutt

U.S. Editorial Team
Editorial Director: Carolyn Jackson
Cover Design: Karen Hudson
Assistant Editor: Mimi George
Grateful acknowledgment is made to Adele Brodkin and Theron Cole.

Photo credits: Brian and Cherry Alexander: p25 (bottom); ANT/NHPA: p51 (top); Kurt Amsler/Jacana: p58–59; Anthony Bannister/NHPA: p84; Des & Jen Bartlett/Bruce Coleman: p20 (bottom); BCI/Britstock-IFA: p35; Alan Beaties/Ardea: p69 (top); Hans & Judy Beste/Ardea: p41 (bottom); Trygue Bolstad/Panos Pictures: p68; John Bracegirdle/Planet Earth Pictures: p78; Jane Burton/Bruce Coleman: p77; Martyn Colbeck/OSF: p30–31; Stephen Dalton/NHPA: p27, p40, p41 (top), p65; E.R. Degginger/OSF: p85 (bottom); Geoff Du Feu/Planet Earth Pictures: p16; Ferrero-Labat/Ardea: p18, p42, p43 (top), p54; Mickey Gibson/OSF: p23 (right); François Gohier/Ardea: p39, p69 (bottom); Howard Hall/OSF: p73; Tony Hallas/Science Photo Library: p81; Martin Harvey/NHPA: p50; Penfa Helo/Bruce Coleman: p26; James Hudnall/Planet Earth Pictures: p86; Images Colour Library: p8–9; M. Isley/Spectrum: p30 (top); Jacana: p62, p76; Peter Johnson/NHPA: p66; Rich Kirchener/NHPA: p51 (left); Stephen Kraseman/NHPA: p24; Jean-Michel Labat/Ardea: p13; Lon E. Lauber/OSF: p67; Michael Leach/OSF: p52; London Scientific Films/OSF: p19; Ken Lucas/Planet Earth Pictures: p22 (left); John Lythgoe/Planet Earth Pictures: p22 (left); Stefan Meyers/Ardea: p43 (bottom), p57; Norbert Wu/Planet Earth Pictures: p60 (bottom); Nuridsany & Perennou/Science Photo Library: p46 (top), p48, p83; Stan Oslinski/OSF: p20 (top); Photo Researchers/OSF: p12; F. Polking/Britstock-IFA: p75 (bottom); Dr. Morely Read/Science Photo Library: p15; Robin Redfern/OSF: p25 (top); J.C. Revy/Science Photo Library: p28; Rev. Ronald Royer/Science Photo Library: p80; David Scharf/Science Photo Library: p10; Jonathon Scott/Planet Earth Pictures: p25 (left), p31, p44–45; Anup Shah/Planet Earth Pictures: p55; Alastair Shay/OSF: p37; Marty Snyderman/Planet Earth Pictures: p72; Tony Stone: p22 (right), p22–23, p32, p44 (left), p45 (right), p58 (top), p58 (bottom left), p63; John Visser/Bruce Coleman: p23 (left); Tom Walker/Jacana: p46 (bottom); Carl Wallace/Bruce Coleman: p17; Kent Wood/Science Photo Library: p85 (top); Zefa: p33 (top, bottom), p47, p51 (right), p70, p74, p75 (top), p87; G. Ziesler/Bruce Coleman: p56.

Produced for Scholastic Inc. by Two-Can Publishing Ltd., 346 Old Street, London, EC1V 9NQ, U.K.
Copyright © 1995 by Scholastic Inc. and Two-Can Publishing Ltd.
All rights reserved. Published by Scholastic Inc.

SCHOLASTIC and associated logos are trademarks and/or registered trademarks of Scholastic Inc.

No part of this publication may be reproduced, or stored in a retrieval system, or transmitted in any form or by any means, electronic, mechanical, photocopying, recording, or otherwise, without written permission of the publisher.
For information regarding permission, write to Scholastic Inc., Attention: Permissions Department, 555 Broadway, New York, NY 10012.

Library of Congress Cataloging-in-Publication Data

    Animals and nature: Scholastic reference
        p.   cm.—(Scholastic first encyclopedia)
    Includes index.
    ISBN 0-590-47524-X (hc)   0-590-47523-1 (pb)
      1. Animals—Encyclopedias, Juvenile. 2. Natural history—
Encyclopedias, Juvenile. [1. Animals—Encyclopedias. 2. Natural
history—Encyclopedias.] I. Scholastic Inc. II. Series.
    QL49.A587   1995
    591'.03—dc20   94-28587
                                  CIP AC

12 11   06 05

Printed in the U.S.A.
First Scholastic trade paperback printing, August 2000

Animals and Nature

SCHOLASTIC REFERENCE

Look it up!

In *Animals and Nature*, there are entries for five important animal classifications (Mammal, Insect, Bird, Fish, and Reptile) and entries on individual animals which best represent these groups. There are also entries for habitats, such as Forest and Desert, as well as the elements, such as Air, Earth, and Water. The entries are organized in alphabetical order. For example, an entry such as Bat is near the front of the book, because B is one of the first letters in the alphabet.

Pronunciation

Some words, such as encyclopedia (en-SY-clo-PEE-dee-a), are difficult to say. To say them correctly, make the sounds in the parentheses after each of the words. The sounds spelled with capital letters are pronounced with more stress, or emphasis.

Cross-references

Above the colored bar on each page there is a list of other entries in this book or the three other books in the *Scholastic First Encyclopedia*, with their book titles. These other entries tell you more about the subject on the page. If there are a lot of entries, the title of the book only is given. Entries in *A First Atlas* are listed by the map headings. You will find more information in the section that follows the map heading given.

Contents

The Contents page at the front of the book lists the main entries, or subjects in the book, and which page they are on.

Glossary

Words in the book that may be difficult to understand are marked in **bold.** The Glossary near the back of the book lists these words and explains what they mean.

Index

The Index at the back of the book is a list of everything mentioned in the book, arranged in alphabetical order, with its page number. If an entry is in *italics*, it means that it is a label on a picture. If the page number only is in *italics*, the entry appears in the main text as well as being a picture label.

Contents

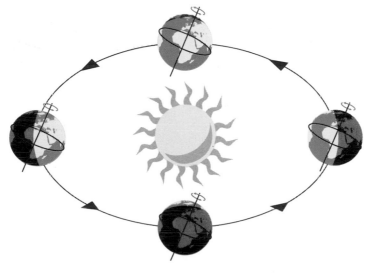

The natural world

The natural world is the part of the world around you that is not made by people. *Animals and Nature* tells you about many of the billions of animals and plants that make their homes in the oceans and on land. It explains how they are **adapted** to their **habitats**, how they are alike and how they are different. The book also tells you about the earth, and what happens on it, underground and undersea, and in the sky above it.

Animal groups
Some animals have soft fur on their bodies. Others have prickles, scales, or slick, wet skin. There are animals that dig, climb, hop, run, swim, or fly. Scientists have put animals into groups to make it easier to study them. Mammals, birds, reptiles, and fish have backbones to give their bodies strength. These animal groups are known as **vertebrates**. Many small creatures, such as insects, have no backbones and are called **invertebrates**.

Nature at work
Mountains, deserts, and forests are part of the natural world. So are fresh-water rivers and lakes, and saltwater oceans. *Animals and Nature* tells you how these natural things are formed and how the weather shapes and changes them.

▶ Hippopotamuses are mammals that live in lakes, rivers, and streams close to the grasslands in parts of Africa. They are the third largest land animals. Only elephants and rhinoceroses are bigger.

Air

Air is a mixture of invisible **gases** that covers the earth in a layer over 400 miles high. This layer is called the **atmosphere**. It provides the **oxygen** that all living things need. During the day, it also protects us from harmful rays from the sun. At night, it acts like a blanket to keep the earth warm.

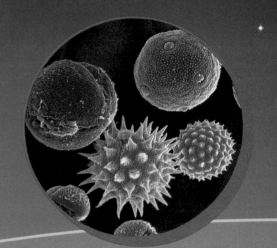

▲ Tiny pollen grains are carried by the air as the wind blows them from plant to plant. This pollen is shown hundreds of times bigger than it really is.

Most birds, bats, and winged insects can fly. Flying is the quickest way to travel long distances, as birds and butterflies do when they **migrate**. It can also help with catching food. Some birds hover above the ground looking for **prey**. Other birds, and bats, eat insects that they catch in flight.

Air contains floating particles of dust, seeds, and even tiny living creatures, as well as gases. Smoke and fumes from factories and cars also mix with the air and **pollute** it.

Plants, land animals, birds, and some sea animals take a gas called oxygen from the air that they breathe. They need it to get **energy** from their food.

ozone
High in the atmosphere there is a layer of air that is rich in a special type of oxygen called ozone. It stops most of the sun's harmful ultraviolet rays from reaching the earth.

We cannot see, smell, or taste air, but we can feel it moving as a breeze, and we can see a balloon or bicycle tire grow bigger as it fills with air.

Water animals breathe oxygen that is part of the water in rivers and seas.

Bat

Bats are small furry mammals with leathery wings. They are the only mammals that can fly. Most bats only fly at night. They rest during the day, hanging upside down in caves, attics, barns, or trees. There are more than 900 kinds of bats, living all over the world, except in very cold places. Some, such as horseshoe bats, are **endangered**.

Most bats have one baby a year. There is no nest for the young bat to sit in, so it clings to its mother's fur or hangs from a rock. Baby bats feed on their mother's milk for about six weeks.

▲ Long-nosed bats use their long tongues to drink sweet nectar from flowers. Many other bats feed on flying insects or catch fish, small birds, and other animals.

Group life

Bats rest by clinging to rocks or twigs with their curved claws. Most bats live in groups called colonies. In cool climates, where there are no insects in winter, bats either **migrate** to a warmer area, or they hibernate. Hibernation is a deep sleep in which the body does not need much **energy**, and therefore little food.

▶ Fruit bats feed on fruit and nectar from flowers. They can have a **wingspan** of nearly 5 feet.

Seeing in the dark

As it flies, a bat makes noises that are too high-pitched for people to hear. These sounds bounce off objects and back to the bat's ears. The echoes they make help the bat to find its way in the dark and tell it where to catch its next insect meal.

The vampire

Vampire bats feed on blood. At night they creep on to the backs of **cattle**, bite through the skin, and suck out blood. Their teeth are so sharp that they can bite without even waking their victims.

Bird

Birds are the only animals with feathers. They all have wings and most can fly. Birds are **vertebrates**. They are warm-blooded, which means their bodies stay at about the same **temperature**, whatever the weather. Young birds hatch from eggs, and adult birds often build a nest to keep the eggs and babies safe. Birds live in every part of the world in forests, deserts, cities, oceans, marshland, and on mountaintops.

Birds build their nests in trees, hedges, buildings, on rocky cliffs, and on the ground. The nests are usually made of twigs, grass, leaves, hair, or mud. Some birds leave their nesting place to migrate, spending the summer in one place and then flying to a warmer home to find food for the winter.

▶ A woodpecker makes its nest in a hole that it digs in the trunk of a tree.

Beaks
Birds have no teeth. Instead they have hard bills, or beaks, which are shaped to suit particular jobs. They are used for collecting food, building nests, and for protection.

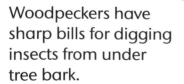

Woodpeckers have sharp bills for digging insects from under tree bark.

Spoonbills move their wide, flat beaks through the water to find **prey**.

Seed-eating birds have small, strong beaks to help them crack seeds.

beak or bill

Feet
Swimming birds have webbed feet, which act like paddles, pushing them through the water. Birds that climb tree trunks have toes which help them to grip. Some birds have very sharp claws, or talons, which they use to catch prey.

swimming bird's foot

climbing bird's foot

foot

wing
Birds' wings are specially shaped for certain kinds of flying. Birds with long, pointed wings are fast flyers, while forest birds have short wings for dodging through trees.

feathers

▶ A feather has a flat vane, made up of hundreds of branches that sit side by side, with a stiff shaft at its center.

See also Flower, Insect

Butterfly

Butterflies are insects that live in almost every part of the world. There are more than fifteen thousand different kinds. They have two pairs of colorful wings and long feelers, or antennae (an-TEN-ee), growing on their heads. They use their antennae for touching and smelling. Butterflies feed on a sugary liquid called nectar, which they collect from flowers.

From caterpillar to butterfly

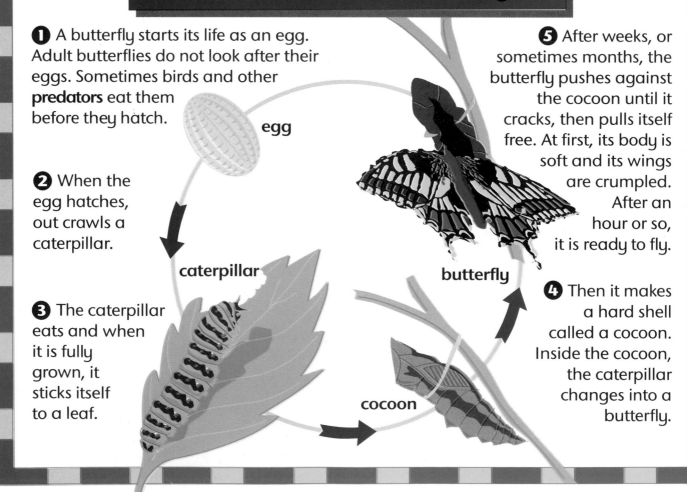

1 A butterfly starts its life as an egg. Adult butterflies do not look after their eggs. Sometimes birds and other **predators** eat them before they hatch.

egg

2 When the egg hatches, out crawls a caterpillar.

caterpillar

3 The caterpillar eats and when it is fully grown, it sticks itself to a leaf.

cocoon

5 After weeks, or sometimes months, the butterfly pushes against the cocoon until it cracks, then pulls itself free. At first, its body is soft and its wings are crumpled. After an hour or so, it is ready to fly.

butterfly

4 Then it makes a hard shell called a cocoon. Inside the cocoon, the caterpillar changes into a butterfly.

antennae   proboscis

Colorful adults

A butterfly's wings are covered with tiny colored scales that give them their wonderful patterns. As butterflies get older, they lose these scales and their colors seem to fade. Most adult butterflies live for only one or two weeks.

▶ A butterfly sucks nectar through a tube called a proboscis (pro-BOS-kiss).

A butterfly's long antennae, or feelers, touch and smell things. They are like tiny sponges that soak up smells from flowers and other insects. Butterfly antennae have knobs on the ends.

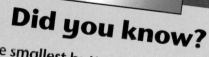

Did you know?

The smallest butterflies are less than half an inch wide, which is about the size of a house fly.

Queen Alexandra's birdwing, the largest butterfly in the world, is 11 inches wide across its wings. That is bigger than a small bird.

Every winter, monarch butterflies in Canada escape the cold by traveling 2,000 miles to Mexico.

▲ These butterflies are hard to see. They are **camouflaged** (CAM-uh-flahjed), which helps them hide from their enemies such as birds and other insects.

Cat

The cat family includes big cats, such as lions and tigers, small wild cats, and **domestic**, or pet cats. All cats are meat-eating mammals and clever hunters, with powerful bodies and sharp claws. They are very good climbers and often live in forests. Cats can be found in most parts of the world, but some kinds are rare because they have been hunted for their fur, or their **habitats** have been destroyed.

Newborn cats cannot see or hear for several days. Their mother protects them, feeds them, and keeps them clean until they can manage alone.

Did you know?

Tigers are the largest members of the cat family. A male tiger can be nearly 40 times heavier and four times taller than a domestic cat.

A cheetah can run up to 70 miles an hour over short distances. It is the fastest land animal in the world.

Cats are not able to taste sweet things.

▲ Young cheetahs are called cubs. Their mother looks after them for over a year, teaching them how to hunt **prey** such as antelope.

Cats have a good sense of smell and sight, and very sharp hearing. Their large ears pick up sounds easily, and each ear can move separately, to catch every little noise. A cat uses its long whiskers to feel its way around.

▶ **All cats whiskers have their own special pattern. No two sets of whiskers are the same.**

Cat sounds

One of the differences between big and small cats is that they have slightly different throats that make different sounds. Most big cats can roar but cannot purr, while small cats can purr but cannot roar.

Most lions live in the grasslands of Africa. Unlike other cats, they live together in groups called prides. The females are usually the hunters, but the males always eat their share of the food first.

Spots and stripes

A tiger's stripes blend in with the tall grasses of its hunting ground. They surprise their pre y by creeping silently forward on soft, padded paws before they pounce.

Many cats' patterned fur coats help them to hide from their prey. Spotted leopards are hard to see among the branches of their forest homes.

Crocodile

Crocodiles are large, fierce reptiles that live in rivers, salt marshes, and swamps in warm parts of the world. They have long, scaly bodies and strong jaws full of sharp teeth. They catch fish, frogs, birds, pigs, antelopes, and even other crocodiles to eat. They use their powerful tails to push themselves through the water when they swim. On land, crocodiles can move quickly on their short legs.

▲ A crocodile lies in wait for its next meal. Only its eyes and nostrils show above the water.

Baby crocodiles hatch from eggs, like baby birds. A mother crocodile lays about 30 eggs in a nest. She covers the eggs with sand or rotting plants to keep them warm, and watches over them. She guards her young until they are old enough to look after themselves.

▲ When the babies hatch they call to their mother. She breaks open the nest and releases her young.

Did you know?

Crocodiles sometimes eat stones to help them **digest** their food. The stones also help them float the right way up.

The salt-water crocodile, the largest in the world, can grow as long as a luxury automobile and weigh as much as five people.

Crocodiles keep on growing throughout their lives.

Daily life

In the morning, crocodiles lie in the sun to warm up. During the hottest part of the day they swim or lie in the mud to keep cool. They hunt in the evening, waiting near a shore or riverbank to catch the animals that come to drink.

The crocodile family

The crocodile family includes alligators, caimans (KAY-mans), and gavials (GAY-vee-uhls). They can usually be recognized by the shape of their jaws, or snouts. An alligator has a broader, more rounded snout than a crocodile. Caimans have very similar snouts to alligators, and gavials have long, thin snouts that are good for catching fish.

crocodile

gavial

alligator

▲ Birds do the work of a toothbrush, cleaning scraps of food and **parasites** from a crocodile's teeth.

21

Desert

A desert is a dry, barren place where rain rarely falls. Some deserts are huge areas of sand. Some are flat, stony **plains** where a few scrubby plants grow. Others are bare, rocky, and mountainous. The hottest deserts are near the **Equator**. Only a few animals and plants can survive the harsh desert climate.

Desert plants often store rainwater that lasts through long dry spells. Some grow only when it rains. Their seeds sprout quickly, and flowers bloom for several days. The plants soon die, but millions of new seeds lie waiting for the next rainfall.

◀ This sidewinder rattlesnake uses its head and tail to support its body as it moves sideways.

▶ A cactus is a desert plant with roots that spread over a wide area, to catch as much rain as possible.

An oasis (oh-AY-sis) is an area in a desert with a supply of water from underground. People grow food there. Date palm trees shade the plants that produce other fruits, vegetables, and grains such as wheat and barley.

◀ In some deserts, sand blown by the wind forms hills called dunes.

▶ Camels are well **adapted** to desert life. The humps on their backs store fat. That way they can keep going for many days without food or water. Their wide, flat feet do not sink into the desert sand.

◀ Scorpions use the poisonous sting at the end of their tails to kill the small desert animals that they hunt.

Dog

Dogs are strong, fast mammals that usually have furry coats and long muzzles. They have powerful teeth and jaws. Dogs are hunters and scavengers. They have weak eyes and rely on their hearing and strong sense of smell. Dogs were the first animals to be tamed by humans, and they have lived and worked with people for thousands of years. The dog family includes foxes, coyotes (ky-O-tees), and jackals.

Did you know?

A dog named Laika became the world's first space traveler. She was sent up in a Russian spacecraft nearly 40 years ago.

The smallest dog is a Chihuahua (chi-WA-wa). It is only about 5 inches tall from its paws to its shoulders. That's about as high as a tin can.

Female dogs have between one and twelve puppies at a time. For the first few days of their lives, the puppies feed on their mother's milk. As they get older, their mother feeds them meat which she has chewed to make it easier to swallow.

Wolves are the largest members of the dog family. They are the **ancestors** of the dogs people keep as pets. Wolves used to be very common, but now they live only in parts of Europe, Asia, and North America that are far away from people.

◀ Wolves often howl to warn others that they are nearby.

Red foxes are found all around the world. They can live on mountains, in deserts, and even in cities. They eat small animals and birds, or scavenge in garbage cans.

▶ Foxes only live in family groups while their young are growing up. At other times, they live alone or in pairs.

Some dogs do useful work for people. Sheepdogs help shepherds to round up large flocks of sheep. Guide dogs help blind people to find their way around.

▲ Most dogs hunt in groups called packs. African wild dogs work together to find and catch food.

Many of today's pet, or **domestic**, dogs look very different from wolves, often because people **bred** them to do special jobs. Terriers are small because they were bred to hunt animals in their underground burrows. Greyhounds are light and fast, for hunting rabbits.

▲ Husky dogs work as a team. They can pull heavy sledges over snow.

Eagle

Eagles are large, powerful hunting birds that are found in most parts of the world. They have broad wings and very good eyesight. Eagles feed on small mammals, birds, or fish, using their sharp talons, or claws, and huge, hooked beaks to grab and tear their **prey**.

Feathering a nest

Eagles live far away from people, at the top of tall trees or high cliffs. They build huge nests called aeries from sticks and leaves.

A female eagle lays two or three eggs. Both parents take turns sitting on them to keep them warm. When they hatch, the parents guard the nest and feed their young, called eaglets.

▼ Eaglets are looked after by their parents until they have gained strength and grown feathers for flying.

◀ The North American bald eagle can fly over 200 miles in a day. It is the national symbol of the United States of America.

▼ Fish eagles search out their prey from the waterside. Then they glide down and hook a wriggling fish in their long talons.

Did you know?

Many eagles return to the same aerie each year, adding new material every time. One aerie weighed as much as two cars and took 35 years to build.

The harpy eagle of Central and South America is one of the world's most powerful birds. It hunts monkeys and other forest animals by tearing them from the branches with its strong talons.

Earth

The earth is a **planet** that is home to a huge range of living things. Its outer surface is a thin layer of hard rock called crust. It is covered with soil, water, and more layers of rock. These form many kinds of land, and different plant and animal **habitats**. The earth's crust changes all the time. Weather gradually breaks up or wears away the surface of the rock, changing the shape of the land very slowly. Earthquakes, landslides, and erupting volcanoes change it much more suddenly.

dung beetle

snail

minerals
Minerals are found in rocks. They include salt, metals such as iron, and gems, or precious stones. **Fuels** such as coal are also found deep underground. They form over a long period of time from the remains of living things.

soil
In many places, the very top layer of the earth is not rock but soil. Soil is a mixture of sand, mud, and stones with the remains of dead plants and animals. These remains add **nutrients** to the soil. Plants use the nutrients to grow, taking them in through their roots.

The earth's crust is made up of different types of rock. Some are formed when molten rock from below the crust comes to the surface and hardens. Others form under the sea, when sand and mud are squashed together on the sea bed.

◀ Rubies are one of the rarest and most precious gems. They are found deep underground, embedded in rock.

beetle

ant

centipede

Some kinds of animals live or shelter in soil. They burrow, mixing the soil and making it finer. Their burrows also let in air. This, in turn, makes the soil a better place for plants to grow.

mole

millipede

fossils
Fossils are often formed when the remains of a dead plant or animal turn gradually to stone, leaving a shape imprinted in the rock. As the earth changes, fossils are buried. When they are found many years later, they can tell us about past life on the earth.

earthworm

29

Elephant

Elephants are the biggest land animals in the world. These mammals have thick, wrinkly gray skin and long noses called trunks. They live in grasslands and forests and feed mainly on grass and the fruit and leaves of trees. There are two main kinds of elephant. One kind lives in Africa and the other in Asia. African elephants are larger and fiercer, with bigger tusks and ears.

▲ Asian elephants are trained to do work. They can lift heavy loads with their strong trunks.

Young elephants are protected by the females in their group, or herd. They stay close by their mothers until they are about ten years old.

▼ A herd of elephants travels many miles in search of food and water.

Elephants use their trunks to smell, to greet one another, and to put food and water into their mouths. They keep cool by flapping their ears to make a breeze. This cools the blood that passes through their ears. They blow out water from their trunks to give themselves a shower.

Big teeth

Elephants' tusks, or long front teeth, are made of ivory. For years, people hunted elephants for this ivory to make jewelry, piano keys, and tool handles. Now it is against the law. Only female Asian elephants do not have tusks.

▶ Elephants have few enemies apart from people. Their size, tough skin, and sharp tusks protect them from other animals.

Did you know?

A mother elephant is pregnant for nearly two years before her baby is born. This is longer than any other mammal.

An elephant's trunk contains over fifty thousand muscles.

The elephant's closest living relative is the rabbit-like hyrax, which is small enough to fit in your pocket.

Farm

A farm is a place where people grow plants and keep animals. Small farms grow just enough to feed farmers and their families. Bigger farms grow more food to sell to other people. Most of our food comes from these. The most common farm animals are **cattle**, sheep, goats, hogs, chickens, and horses.

Some farmers grow plants but do not keep animals. The most important food plants are grains, such as wheat and rice. Farmers also grow sugar, beans, fruit, vegetables, and cotton for making clothes.

▼ This farmer is using a machine called a combine harvester to cut barley.

Farm animals

Cattle are kept for their milk, or for meat. They need good, juicy grass to eat, and shelter from bad weather. Sheep are raised for their thick, warm wool and their meat. They also eat grass but, unlike cattle, they can live on steep hillsides. There are huge sheep farms in Australia, Russia, China, and New Zealand.

now picture this

From time to time, huge swarms of insects called locusts destroy crops. They eat huge amounts and sometimes there are so many locusts that they block out the sunlight.

▶ These horses are helping to round up cattle. Workers can easily cover every part of a large ranch on horseback.

Hogs, or pigs, are raised for their meat and skin. They eat almost anything. Goats provide milk and meat, and they can find food on even the poorest land. Chickens are raised for their eggs or for meat. They usually eat grain. Horses, donkeys, and mules are usually kept to do work on a farm. Big farms rely on tractors and other machines.

▶ Rice needs plenty of water as it grows, so people often plant it in flooded fields.

33

Fish

Fish are animals that live in water. Most have fins and a tail, which they use for swimming. All fish are **vertebrates** and most are cold-blooded, so their bodies are usually at the same **temperature** as the water around them. Fish eat plants and water animals, including other fish, and their young almost always hatch from eggs. There are thousands of different kinds of fish living in seas, oceans, rivers, and lakes in almost every part of the world.

swim bladder
Some fish have a small bag of gas called a swim bladder inside their bodies, to stop them from sinking.

gills
Like all animals, fish need **oxygen** to live. They breathe oxygen from water, which they gulp in through their mouths. It passes over body parts called gills, which take the oxygen from the water and pass it into the fish's blood.

▲ **Goldfish belong to a group of fish called carp.**

fin

▶ Most fish hatch from eggs. Some kinds lay thousands of eggs at a time, and leave them unprotected. Many never hatch. Some fish build nests for their eggs and guard their young.

tail
Most fish swing their tails and bend their bodies from side to side to swim forward. Long, thin fish, such as eels, wriggle their bodies. Others, such as rays, flap their large fins like wings.

scales
The skin of most fish is covered with protective scales.

Flower

A flower is the part of a plant that makes seeds. Later, the seeds will grow into new plants. Flowers are often bright and colorful and many have a pleasant smell. Many grasses and trees have small, green flowers without a smell.

1 In the middle of a flower is a case that holds the flower's eggs. Around it are tiny stalks, or stamens, covered in dust called pollen. Above the egg case is a sticky stigma.

2 To make a seed, pollen from one stamen must land on a stigma. This is called pollination. It may occur from one flower to another or on the same flower.

3 A pollen tube grows from the pollen on the stigma towards the egg case. Sperm from the pollen move through the tube to fertilize the egg.

stamen

egg case

On the move

Flowers are pollinated in different ways. Some produce millions of tiny, light pollen grains that are carried by the wind. Others attract insects with their color and scent. Flowers make a sugary liquid called nectar. While insects drink the nectar, pollen sticks to their bodies and the insects carry it from flower to flower.

Busy bees

Bees pollinate more flowers than any other insect. They make nectar into honey and collect pollen to make "bee bread" to feed young bees, or larvae (LAR-vee), in their nest or hive.

stigma

▲ A bee's body is covered with tiny hairs that pick up pollen as the bee brushes against the flower's stamens.

petal

stem

From flowers to fruits

Once a flower has been pollinated, the petals wither and fall off. The eggs grow into seeds. The egg case becomes a fruit, which protects the seeds and helps them to spread far away from the parent plant. Some seeds are blown by the wind. Others travel inside and pass through the bodies of animals that eat the fruit.

Forest

A forest is a large area of land covered by trees. There are forests in different parts of the world. The trees provide food and shelter for many other living things. Nearly three-quarters of all land animals and plants live in forests.

Coniferous forests stretch in a huge band across the north of Russia and North America. The winters are long and cold, while the summers are short but warm. Most of the trees are conifers, such as pine and spruce, that produce naked seeds in cones and remain green year-round.

fir tree

beech tree

oak tree

lichen

moss

Deciduous forests contain broad-leaved trees that lose their leaves in the fall, such as beeches and maples. Their branches stay bare through the winter. In spring, flowers cover the forest floor before new leaves grow on the trees and block out their light. Some forests are mixed with coniferous and deciduous trees.

Tropical forests grow near the Equator. They contain hundreds of different kinds of trees with tall, thin trunks and tops that spread out to catch as much light as possible. Some tropical forests have a wet and a dry season, while tropical rain forests are hot and wet all year round.

tapang tree

maple tree

liana

palm tree

► Leaf-cutter ants use their powerful jaws to cut pieces from forest plants.

orchid

mushrooms

tree fern

poisonous toadstools

39

Frog

Frogs are amphibians (am-FIB-eans), animals that spend part of their lives in water and part on land. As adults, frogs live near ponds and streams where they can keep their smooth skins moist. They have large eyes on the sides of their heads which allow them to see in all directions. They can jump a long way on their strong back legs. Frogs live all over the world.

▲ A toad looks much like a frog, but it has a dry, bumpy skin and spends most of its life on land.

From tadpole to frog

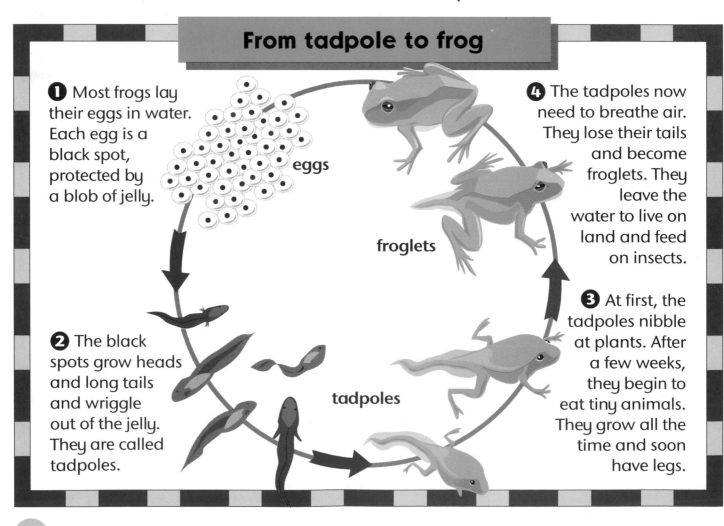

❶ Most frogs lay their eggs in water. Each egg is a black spot, protected by a blob of jelly.

eggs

❷ The black spots grow heads and long tails and wriggle out of the jelly. They are called tadpoles.

tadpoles

froglets

❹ The tadpoles now need to breathe air. They lose their tails and become froglets. They leave the water to live on land and feed on insects.

❸ At first, the tadpoles nibble at plants. After a few weeks, they begin to eat tiny animals. They grow all the time and soon have legs.

Trapping food

A frog sits quite still, waiting for passing insects. In a flash, it flicks out its sticky tongue. The insect sticks on and is flipped back into the frog's mouth.

▶ A tree frog uses its muscular back legs to jump from one leaf to another.

Male frogs call noisily to attract females. Each kind of frog has its own special call. Some puff out their throats into a bubble, and croak. Others peep, and some even bleat like goats.

▼ Tree frogs have sticky toes to help them cling to trees.

Did you know?

Rainforest people tip their arrows using the poison from the deadly South American arrow-poison frog. One frog has enough poison to tip 50 arrows, and each arrow can kill a deer or a big cat, such as a jaguar.

Most large frogs can push their eyes out of their sockets to make more space in their mouths when they eat.

Giraffe

Giraffes are mammals with very long necks and legs that make them the world's tallest animals. They live in small groups in the grasslands of Africa, feeding on twigs, leaves, and fruit. Adult giraffes have few enemies but they are sometimes attacked by lions. They defend themselves by kicking out with their strong front legs.

Most giraffes have just one baby at a time. Young giraffes can stand up on their thin, wobbly legs an hour after they are born. They stay close to their mothers at first, because they cannot run fast and are in danger from lions, leopards, crocodiles, and hyenas.

Giraffes use their lips and tongues to collect their food from scattered trees. Their long necks help them to reach branches up to 20 feet above the ground.

◀ A giraffe's tongue is nearly one and a half feet long, and tough enough to eat thorny plants.

▼ Giraffes' long legs help them run at speeds of up to 40 miles an hour.

Did you know?

Giraffes sleep standing up. They spend only 20 minutes asleep each night.

To keep out sand and dust, a giraffe can close its nostrils completely.

Male giraffes can be 18 feet tall. That is almost as high as four men standing on each other's shoulders.

Now you see me ...

A giraffe's coat is covered with brown and white markings. Every giraffe has its own special pattern. When the animal stands under trees, its markings look like the dappled shadows of twigs and branches. It is so well **camouflaged** (CAM-uh-flahjed) you can barely see the giraffe.

Tests of strength

Giraffes are usually peaceful animals, but males sometimes fight between themselves. They swing their heavy heads in a kind of slow dance. The sound of their blows is so loud that it can be heard from far away.

▶ To drink, giraffes spread their front legs wide apart and lower their necks between them towards the water.

Grass

Grasses are one of the most common plants in the world. They are tough and can grow almost anywhere, from the freezing Arctic **tundra** to the hot, dry **plains** of Africa and South America. There are many kinds of grass. Rice, wheat, corn, oats, and barley are all grasses and important foods for people and for most farm animals.

▼ Ostriches are grassland birds that cannot fly. They rely on their powerful legs to run from danger.

There are huge areas of grassland on every continent except Antarctica. Most are flat plains where little rain falls. There are two main types. **Temperate** grasslands are called prairies in some areas and pampas, or steppes, in other places. **Tropical** grasslands are known as savannahs.

▲ Weaver birds
build their hanging nests
using grass and twigs.

▲ Zebras and wildebeests roam the African savannah.
They are hunted by lions, leopards, and hyenas.

Savannahs are covered with clumps of tall
grasses, scattered trees, and bushes. They are
full of animal life. Meat-eating predators hunt
the large plant-eating mammals that **graze**.
Flocks of birds feed on insects and on the fruits
and seeds of savannah plants.

Grassland alert

In some areas, grasslands
are being taken over for
farming, making life hard
for animals that live there.
If land is plowed or grazed
too often, the grasses die,
and the soil is quickly
washed or blown away.

45

Ice

Ice is frozen water. It is hard and clear, and cold to the touch. Tiny air bubbles trapped inside it often make it look white. If it is heated, ice melts and becomes liquid again.

The coldest places on Earth are the Arctic region around the North Pole and the continent of Antarctica at the South Pole. The oceans are usually covered with ice. Winter is especially cold and dark. Fierce, icy winds bring terrible snowstorms. In the Antarctic mountains, huge rivers of ice and snow, called glaciers, flow slowly down the mountainsides. Some of them travel right down to the sea.

▲ Snowflakes come in an almost endless variety of patterns.

All kinds of ice

Snow and hail are types of ice. Snow is made when water **vapor** freezes to make ice crystals. Hailstones are frozen raindrops. In cold weather, the tops of puddles, ponds, and lakes turn to ice.

▼ Polar bears roll on the icy ground to dry their thick fur after swimming.

Icebergs

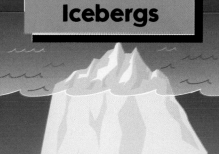

In the polar regions, large chunks break off glaciers and sea ice and form icebergs that float away on the ocean currents. The largest part of an iceberg is hidden underwater. Only one-tenth shows above the surface.

▲ Antarctic animals depend on the ocean for their food. Penguins dive off the ice to hunt for fish to eat.

In the summer, birds arrive in the Arctic from the south to nest and raise their young. Flowers bloom, and attract butterflies. Some creatures, such as walruses and seals, stay all year. They swim in the ocean and eat fish and other sea creatures. They are hunted by male polar bears, while the females spend the winter in snow dens with their cubs.

The frozen south

Much of Antarctica is so cold that few creatures can live there. Some kinds of penguins stay all year. Seals and whales are summer visitors.

Insect

There are more kinds of insects than any other animals. They live all over the world, from high mountains to dry deserts. Insects are small **invertebrate** animals with three parts to their bodies and three pairs of legs. Most have two sets of wings and can fly in search of food or away from enemies. Their young hatch from eggs.

Insects protect themselves in all kinds of ways. Some look just like their surroundings, which helps them hide from their enemies. Others attack by biting or stinging. Dangerous insects are often brightly colored, which warns enemies to stay away.

head

antenna
Insects find their food by seeing, smelling, and touching. Some have long antennae (an-TEN-ee), which they use to feel and smell. Most insects do not have ears. Instead, they use tiny hairs on their bodies to pick up sound **vibrations** from the air.

eye

thorax

◀ Many insects have huge eyes. These are called compound eyes because they are made up of many separate **lenses**.

leg

Insect groups

Most insects live alone, but some, such as bees, termites, and ants, live in big groups and help each other. Each member of the group has a job to do. There is one queen in a nest and she lays eggs. She is looked after by workers that gather food or guard the nest.

termite nest

skeleton

An insect's **skeleton** is on the outside of its body. It is a hard case that protects the insect.

abdomen

Life cycles

When insect eggs hatch, the young often look nothing like their parents. Their bodies go through a series of changes, called metamorphosis (met-uh-MORF-uh-sis).

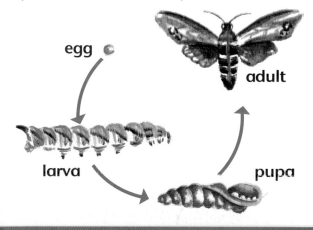

egg

adult

larva

pupa

wing

▲ Wasps are very common insects in many parts of the world. There are over 17,000 different kinds.

Kangaroo

Kangaroos are plant-eating animals with large ears, strong back legs, short front legs, and long tails. They live mainly in the grasslands of Australia, but some are also found in its forests and deserts. Kangaroos can travel fast by hopping along on their back legs, using their tails to help them balance. A female kangaroo has a big pouch on the front of her body where her baby, or joey, grows. Animals with a pouch for their young are called marsupials (mar-SOOP-e-als).

A joey's journey

Kangaroos have one joey at a time. At first the joey is about the size of a human thumb.

A joey spends about six months inside the pouch, but drinks milk from its mother until it is a year old.

When a joey is born, it makes its way to the mother's pouch, crawling through her fur and clinging on tightly.

▶ A joey will jump into its mother's pouch at the first sign of danger.

There are many kinds of kangaroos. Some of the smaller ones are known as wallabies. The biggest are red kangaroos, which have reddish-brown fur and are the same height as a tall man. They live in hot, dry areas, in groups called mobs. They spend their days resting in the shade, licking their front legs to cool off. They feed in the evening, when it is cooler.

► Male kangaroos fight one another to decide who is boss. The winner becomes the leader of the group.

◄ A red kangaroo can run up to 30 miles an hour. As it runs, it holds up its thick tail to help it balance.

▼ Koalas are also marsupials. A baby koala spends its first six months in its mother's pouch and the next six riding on her back.

Mammal

Mammals are a group of **vertebrates** that includes not only zebras and whales but people as well. Most mammal babies are born live, not hatched, and get milk from their mothers. They are warm-blooded, so their bodies stay nearly the same **temperature** all the time. There are mammals living on land, underground, in the water, and in the air.

tail

◄ All mammals have hair on their skin. Some have a thick, furry coat, and others have just a few whiskers.

All mammals breathe air that goes down into their lungs. The air usually enters a mammal's body through nostrils at the end of its nose.

Sea mammals
Most sea mammals have flippers instead of legs. The flippers help them to swim.

seal

hoof

mane

striped coat

Teeth

Mammals have different kinds of teeth and jaws depending on their food. Most eat plants, some eat both meat and plants, and others eat only meat.

Plant-eating mammals have flat-topped teeth for grinding food.

plant-eater's jaw

Meat-eating mammals have sharp teeth for tearing food.

meat-eater's jaw

baby

Young mammals are often nearly helpless when they are first born. They need more care from their parents than other kinds of animals do.

◄ Zebras are members of the horse family. Like many mammals, they have patterns on their fur to help them hide from their enemies. Their stripes make them difficult to see in tall grass.

Monkey

There are about 200 different kinds of monkeys and they are all mammals. Most live in the forests of Africa, Asia, or Central and South America. They have long arms and legs for leaping and swinging through the trees. They use their hands, feet, and long tails to grip the branches and help them balance. Some of those that live on the ground have shorter tails. Monkeys feed on leaves, fruit, flowers, roots, small animals, or eggs.

Did you know?

The macaque monkeys that live in the high mountains of Japan stay warm by bathing in hot springs. They even cook their vegetables in the hot water.

Many monkeys make a fresh bed of leaves and branches every night.

A baboon's huge, strong teeth are a powerful weapon. A male baboon can kill a leopard.

▲ Most monkeys have one baby at a time. A young baboon travels about by clinging to its mother's fur, until it is old enough to get around alone.

Follow the leaders

All monkeys live in groups and many kinds, such as baboons, live in large groups with more than one leader. The leaders keep the group together, protect it against enemies, and stop group members from fighting among themselves.

▶ A spider monkey swings from branch to branch using its long tail as an extra arm.

Danger calls

Monkeys "talk" to each other in different ways. Some make signals with their hands, or make faces. Vervet monkeys have a special kind of screech to warn others that an eagle is near. When they hear the call, the monkeys drop to the ground. Another kind of screech means "leopard!" This sends the monkeys running into the trees.

▲ Many monkeys call out when an enemy comes close, to let other monkeys know they may be in danger.

The apes

orang-utan

gibbon

A closely related group of animals, called apes, includes chimpanzees, gibbons, gorillas, and orang-utans. Apes are a lot like monkeys except that they have no tail and are often bigger and more intelligent.

gorilla

chimpanzee

Mountain

Mountains are high hills with steep slopes. They rise above the land around them. Mountains are usually found in long lines called ranges. There are mountain ranges all over the world, even under the sea.

▲ In the Andes Mountains in South America, huge condors fly overhead looking for dead animals, or carrion, to eat.

Making mountains

Some mountain ranges take millions of years to form. Rocks push slowly together when the earth's crust moves. As they push, they curve upwards into huge folds, which become mountains.

Volcanoes are holes, or vents, that go down through the earth's hard crust to the hot, liquid layer below. When some volcanoes erupt, liquid rock and ash pour out and pile up around the volcano, forming a mountain in just a few years.

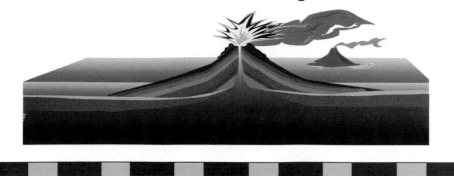

At the tops of the highest mountains there is very little **oxygen** and the air is cold. The peaks are often covered with ice and snow. Trees grow on the lower slopes of a mountain, but higher up, above the tree line, it is too cold and dry for them to survive. Only grasses and a few other tough plants can live this high up.

▼ Ibex are a kind of mountain goat. Their sharp hooves are split to help them grip rocky mountain slopes.

Mountain life

Animals that live on high mountains have hairy coats or thick feathers to keep them warm. Bigger animals have to be good at climbing. Food is a problem for mountain animals. In winter, plant-eaters such as mountain goats and sheep have to go lower down the mountain to find food. Small animals, such as marmots and Himalayan pikas, spend the winter sleeping underground to save **energy**. Cougars, or mountain lions, must go down the mountain for their **prey**.

57

See also Earth, Fish, Water; A FIRST ATLAS

Ocean

Oceans and seas cover nearly three-quarters of the earth's surface and contain most of its water. Billions of years ago, life on Earth began in the oceans. Today, they contain thousands of different sea creatures, from tiny floating plankton to huge whales.

▲ Surfers use ocean waves to carry them towards the shore.

The ocean's salty water is always moving. It is stirred up by the Earth's spinning movement and by winds blowing over it. These movements make huge circular **currents** that carry cold water to warm parts of the world and warm water to cold parts.

The wind blows the surface of the ocean into waves. These waves can travel thousands of miles before they die out or reach land. As they get near the land, waves grow taller and thinner. Then they topple over and break on the shore.

◄ This fangtooth lives in the deepest, darkest part of the ocean. It has special body parts that make light.

now picture this

Enormous tidal waves, which are caused by earthquakes on the ocean floor, can travel up to 500 miles per hour. That's nearly twice as fast as a racing car.

Ocean life: plankton

Wherever there are enough **nutrients**, tiny plants grow in the ocean and drift with the current. Small animals eat the plants, and drift with them. Together, these plants and animals are known as plankton. Small fish and other sea creatures eat plankton. Sea birds, bigger fish, and seals feed on the plankton-eaters. Without plankton there would be no life in the ocean.

▲ Multicolored coral reefs are made by tiny animals called polyps (POL-ips) that leave their shells behind when they die. When new polyps grow on the old shells, the reef becomes larger.

Octopus

Octopuses belong to a group of animals called mollusks. They live in the world's warm oceans. Their soft, boneless bodies have a tough covering called a mantle to protect them and give them shape. Octopuses have eight arms, or tentacles, which they use to catch mussels, lobsters, shrimp, clams, and crabs. They use their hard, beaklike jaws to crack open shells, and to pull out and cut up the food.

A female octopus lays thousands of eggs in a "nursery" in the rocks. She cares for the eggs and cleans them, spraying them with jets of water until they are ready to hatch. She never leaves them, not even to eat, for about two months.

▲ The tentacles of an octopus are covered with strong suckers made of muscle.

Octopuses use their tentacles to grip rocks or hold on to **prey**. If an octopus loses a tentacle, it simply grows a new one. Giant octopuses wrap their tentacles tightly around their prey and shoot poison into the animal from their mouths. Then they cut into it with their beaks.

now picture this

Giant octopuses can be up to 28 feet long, from the tip of one tentacle to the tip of the opposite tentacle.

▲ A female octopus can lay up to 180,000 eggs at one time.

An octopus has three hearts which pump blood through its body. It breathes through gills, like a fish. It can even change color to match its surroundings. The color changes help the octopus to hide in the rocks or to startle its enemies. An octopus also defends itself by squirting black liquid at an attacker. The liquid forms a thick cloud in the water, hiding the octopus while it escapes.

Traveling backward

Octopuses swim by sucking water into their bodies. Then they pump out the water through an opening under their heads. This makes them shoot backward.

Panda

A giant panda is a large, furry, black-and-white mammal. Pandas belong to the same family as bears, but are very rare. In the wild, giant pandas are found only in the cold mountain areas of China. They live in bamboo forests, and spend much of their time eating. Their main food is the bamboo plant.

A female panda gives birth to one or two tiny white cubs at a time. They are born in caves or holes in trees. They look more like mice than pandas, and at first they are helpless so their mother cradles them to keep them safe.

▲ Giant pandas use their sharp claws to help them hold on when they climb trees. They hide from enemies among the branches.

Other bears

Most bears live in cool northern parts of the world. Like pandas, they have large heads, no tails, and thick, shaggy coats to keep them warm. Their back legs are short and their front legs are powerful, with sharp claws. They cannot see or hear well, but their sense of smell is very good. Many bears hibernate, spending the winter asleep in a den.

spectacled bear

grizzly bear

black bear

▲ Giant pandas hold bamboo stalks in their front paws as they munch. They have an extra pad on each paw, which they use like a thumb to help them grip the bamboo.

Reptile

Reptiles include turtles, lizards, snakes, and crocodiles. They are all **vertebrates** that are cold-blooded, so the **temperature** of their bodies is the same as the air around them. Most young reptiles hatch from eggs. There are reptiles everywhere on Earth, except in Antarctica and in the coldest oceans. Most are meat-eaters and feed on any animals they can catch.

Reptiles make sure they never get too hot or too cold. They lie in the sun to warm up and cool down by creeping into the shade.

tongue
Reptiles have long, sticky tongues for trapping the insects they eat.

scaly skin
Many reptiles shed their skin several times a year when it wears out. A new layer of scales grows underneath the old one and when the reptile is ready, it simply rubs the old skin away.

All snakes are reptiles. Some have a poisonous bite, which they use to kill their **prey**.

cottonmouth

python

Pythons squeeze prey by wrapping themselves tightly around it.

▲ Lizards are closely related to snakes. Unlike snakes, most lizards have legs.

▶ Reptiles can go without water for a long time. Their scaly skin stops them from drying out.

claw-like feet for gripping

egg
Most reptiles hatch from eggs. The female lays her eggs in a hole in a tree or in the ground, and they hatch when the sun warms them. Some kinds of reptiles give birth to live young.

Seal

Seals are mammals. They are perfectly formed for swimming, with smooth, **streamlined** bodies and large flippers, like paddles. Most seals live in the cold oceans of the world. A thick layer of fat called blubber keeps them warm. They feed on sea creatures such as fish,octopus, and shrimp.

Most seals go ashore to have their babies, or pups. They crowd together noisily in huge groups. There are sometimes thousands on one stretch of beach. Each mother has to protect her pup from being squashed!

◀ Fur seals have a soft coat under their thick, rough outer layer of fur.

ice

lair

entrance to lair

▲ Not all seals are born on land. Ringed seals give birth to their pups in icy shelters, or lairs, above the Arctic Ocean.

ocean

Some kinds of seals, such as the harbor seal, are very clumsy on land. They can only move by wriggling their bodies over the ground. Other seals, such as the sea lion, can walk on their flippers.

Dry swimmer
Fur seals have thick, hairy coats. Their fur is made waterproof by oil from their skin, so they can swim without getting their skin wet.

Underwater chase

Seals have whiskers, which help them to pick up the movement of fish in the water. Then the chase begins. Leopard seals are fierce hunters. They hunt penguins by waiting for them near the water's edge.

Walruses are large seals with long whiskers and tusks that live in cold northern places. They use their tusks to cut breathing holes in the ice and sometimes to help pull themselves along. The male walrus with the biggest tusks is usually in charge of a group. Walruses eat shellfish and other creatures that live on the ocean floor, using their whiskers to find food in the dark, murky water.

▶ When walruses leave the sea to lie on ice or rocks, they often pile on top of each other in a big heap.

Seashore

The seashore is where the land meets the sea. In some places, it is a sandy or pebbly beach sloping gently towards the water. In other places, the shore is steep and rocky. In some warm parts of the world, forests of mangrove trees grow at the edge of the sea.

Twice a day, all over the world, the sea rises up the shoreline and then falls back down. This movement is called a tide. It is caused by a strong pull from the sun and moon. Tides make seashore life hard for many creatures. They may be pounded by waves breaking on the shore as the tide comes in. When it goes out, they may be uncovered and dry out if it is hot or freeze if there are cold winds.

▼ Creatures such as lobworms burrow into the sand or mud on the seashore. At low tide, birds come to feed on these animals.

Rock pools

As the tide goes out, pools of sea water are left in dips between the rocks. They are cut off from the waves until the tide rises again, so they provide a calm, sheltered home for many plants and animals.

Limpets, barnacles, and many kinds of shellfish stick themselves firmly to the rocks.

shellfish

seaweed

starfish

Some sea animals look like plants. Sea anemones (a-NEM-oh-nees) use their sticky tentacles for catching tiny fish and other creatures.

crab

sea anemone

Seaweed clings to the rocks. Crabs, winkles, and snails tuck themselves away in the cracks beneath.

Season

In many parts of the world, the weather changes throughout the year. These changes are called the seasons.

Some places have four seasons. These are spring, summer, fall, and winter. Other parts of the world have only one or two seasons. Many tropical places are hot all year with a dry season with no rain, and a wet season when winds bring rain from the ocean.

▲ During the wet season in Asia, from April to October, a strong wind called a monsoon brings very heavy rains.

Why seasons happen

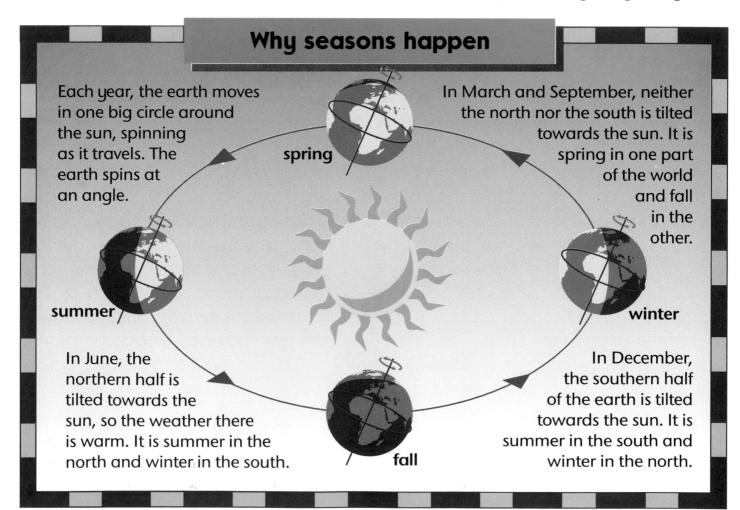

Each year, the earth moves in one big circle around the sun, spinning as it travels. The earth spins at an angle.

spring

In March and September, neither the north nor the south is tilted towards the sun. It is spring in one part of the world and fall in the other.

summer

In June, the northern half is tilted towards the sun, so the weather there is warm. It is summer in the north and winter in the south.

fall

winter

In December, the southern half of the earth is tilted towards the sun. It is summer in the south and winter in the north.

Changing with the seasons

Plants and animals around the world change their lives with the seasons. In spring, seeds grow, buds appear and open, and many animals give birth to young. By summer, most plants are in full flower. Animals grow, too. Tadpoles become frogs, caterpillars become butterflies, and young birds learn to fly.

▶ Dormice hibernate during the winter. They live off the fat stored in their bodies.

In the fall, plants produce fruits and seeds. The leaves of some trees change color and fall to the ground. Many birds fly to warmer lands. In winter, many plants die or stop growing. Some animals, such as bears and bats, sleep all winter to save **energy**.

◀ In places that have a wet season and a dry season, plants like this cactus can survive many months without rain. When the first rains come, everything bursts into life.

71

See also Fish; A FIRST ATLAS Australia and New Zealand; ALL ABOUT PEOPLE Bone

Shark

Sharks are meat-eating fish. They feed on other fish or sea mammals such as seals, sea lions, and dolphins. Most sharks are found in the warm oceans of the world, close to the **Equator**. They have smooth, **streamlined** bodies for speeding through the water. Their **skeletons** are made of cartilage, a strong, flexible **substance** found inside your nose.

Most shark pups are born live from their mothers' bodies. They look just like tiny adults. Once the pups are born they must look after themselves. Sometimes their parents eat them!

▲ Great white sharks use their mouths like giant traps. They close rows of razor-sharp teeth around their **prey**. Then they roll over and tear out huge chunks of meat. They sometimes attack swimmers.

Did you know?

Sharks must keep moving all the time, or they will sink! Most other fish stay afloat using their swim bladder, which is like a gas-filled bag inside them. Sharks do not have swim bladders.

Although it looks smooth, a shark's skin is covered in thousands of tiny toothlike scales. Sailors once used it as sandpaper to scrub the decks of their ships!

Sharks have several rows of teeth. When a tooth is worn out or lost, a new one grows in its place. Some kinds of sharks have very sharp or pointed teeth. Others have flat-topped grinding teeth.

▲ Blue sharks are very fast swimmers, reaching speeds of over 40 miles per hour.

▼ Hammerhead sharks have a flattened head. Their eyes and nostrils are positioned at the ends of the "hammer."

▼ Spotted carpet sharks look just like rocks covered with seaweed. They lie on the sea bed, waiting to grab small fish.

▲ Thresher sharks use their long tails to round up and beat fish such as herrings and pilchards before eating them.

Sharks are very clever hunters. They can see quite well, but they also use their senses of smell and hearing to help them find food. Sharks can hear a human swimmer nearly half a mile away.

Shell

A shell is a hard, protective case. Snails, tortoises, and many sea creatures have shells to protect their soft bodies. Most seashells you find on the beach once belonged to a group of animals called mollusks. They live in oceans all over the world. Different kinds of shells also protect the eggs of birds and some reptiles.

One shell or two?

Some mollusks have a single shell, and others have two shells joined by a kind of hinge. Single-shelled mollusks are called gastropods and they include land and freshwater snails. Most gastropods have shells that grow in a spiral.

Mollusks with two shells are called bivalves. They include clams, oysters, and mussels, and usually cling on to rocks or bury themselves in sand or mud. They filter tiny pieces of food from the water they suck through their shells.

Adult turtles, tortoises, and terrapins are the only reptiles with shells. They have bony skeletons inside their bodies as well. Tortoises live on land and have high, domed shells. Terrapins and turtles have much flatter shells to help them move easily through water. Terrapins live in fresh water, and most turtles live in the sea.

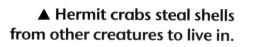

▲ Hermit crabs steal shells from other creatures to live in.

▼ When a baby bird is ready to hatch, it uses a special "egg tooth" on its beak to break open the hard eggshell.

Other shells

Nuts are actually large seeds protected by a shell. Coconuts, acorns, and chestnuts all have hard shells to stop animals from eating their seeds.

▼ A tortoise protects itself from **predators** by pulling its legs and head inside its shell.

Spider

Spiders belong to a group of animals called arachnids (a-RAK-nids). They have eight legs, but no wings or antennae (an-TEN-ee). There are tens of thousands of different kinds of spiders. They live all over the world, on mountains, in forests, deserts, caves, and even under the water. Most eat insects and some trap their food in webs. Others, called hunting spiders, chase or pounce on their **prey**.

Baby spiders, called spiderlings, are born from eggs. Some travel around on their mother's back. Others are carried on the wind, at the end of a fine silk thread.

Spinners and weavers

All spiders spin lines of silk. They use the silk to build nests, make webs and traps to catch prey, wrap up their prey, and protect their eggs. The silk is also used to help a spider travel long distances and as a "lifeline" to save a spider if it falls or to let it hang in mid-air until danger passes.

▲ Tarantula spiderlings hatch from a silky egg sac.

Web trapping

Web-building spiders hang lines of sticky silk in bushes, trees, or fences. They add more and more threads until a net is formed. Insects get caught in the net, which is often sticky. Then the spider attacks its prisoner.

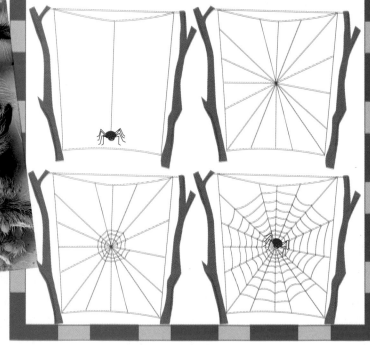

Raft spiders hunt insects, tadpoles, and small fish. They tap the water's surface with their front feet to trick fish into thinking a fly has landed.

▶ A raft spider waits for a fish to swim near, and then grabs the prey in its jaws.

Did you know?

Jumping spiders can leap over 40 times their own body length. They sometimes jump off buildings to catch insects as they fly past.

Tarantulas can measure 10 inches across, enough to cover a small dinner plate!

Bolas spiders spin lines of silk with sticky blobs at the end. They swing them at passing insects to catch them.

Water spiders spend most of their time underwater. They build bell-shaped webs which they fill with air bubbles that can last for several months.

▶ Black widow spiders live in North America. They are one of the few kinds with a poisonous bite that can harm people.

Male spiders are much smaller than females, which sometimes mistake the males for insects and gobble them up! A male wolf spider signals to a female by waving his legs to tell her not to attack.

Tree

A tree is a woody plant with a single stem. Trees are one of the biggest living things on Earth, and they live the longest. A tree has three main parts. They are the crown, the trunk, and the roots.

Broad-leaved trees such as oaks and maples have wide, flat leaves, which many lose for part of the year. Their seeds grow inside the flowers and fruits on the tree.

Cone-bearing trees or **conifers**, such as pines and firs, have thin, hard needles instead of leaves. Their seeds grow inside cones. They can live in much colder places than broad-leaved trees.

flycatcher

Tree houses

Trees provide food and shelter for many other living things. Plants live on the branches or climb up the trunk, and **fungi** grow on the bark. Climbing and flying animals live among the branches, eating flowers, fruits, or seeds. Some munch leaves, or nibble at wood or bark. Others eat the insects that live on trees.

deer

◀ A woodpecker uses its sharp beak to make a hole in a tree trunk, where it builds its nest.

tru

poisonous toadstools

crown

squirrel

Crown

The crown is the top part of a tree, which is divided into many branches, each covered in leaves. The leaves make the tree's food.

How leaves make food

Like all plants, trees make food from water and a **gas** called carbon dioxide. They take carbon dioxide from the air and soak up water through their roots.

sunlight

carbon dioxide

water

leaf makes food for the tree

Leaves contain a special **chemical** called chlorophyll (CLOR-o-fill), which can catch **energy** from the sunlight. Trees use this energy to turn the carbon dioxide and water into food.

Trunk

The trunk of the tree is its stem, which supports the crown. As a tree grows older, its trunk grows thicker. The outer covering is a layer of tough bark, which protects the thin layer of living wood beneath.

Roots

A tree's roots are spread out as far below the ground as the branches spread above. They hold it firmly in the ground and also soak up water from the soil.

◀ If you count the number of rings in the trunk of a tree that has been cut down, you can tell its age. This tree is 14.

roots

chipmunk

Universe

Scientists believe the universe contains everything that exists. The sun, the moon, the **planets**, and all the stars are part of the universe. It reaches farther than scientists can see with their most powerful telescopes.

▲ A **comet** travels on its own special path around the sun. Its tail can be as long as 100 million miles.

The solar system

A group of nine known planets, including Earth, travels around the sun in a huge ring, or orbit. It is called the solar system and is surrounded by space, where there is no air to breathe and things are usually huge distances apart.

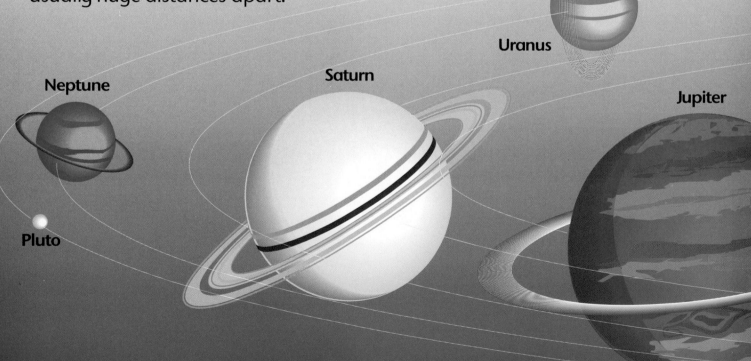

Uranus

Saturn

Jupiter

Neptune

Pluto

Stars and galaxies

The **stars** that we see in the sky at night are burning balls of **gas**, like the sun. They are so far away that they seem very tiny and faint. Our sun is one of a group of millions of stars called the Milky Way. A huge group of stars is called a galaxy.

▶ This giant spiral galaxy is called the Andromeda Galaxy.

The sun is a star, a great ball of glowing gases, which gives us light and warmth. It is many times bigger than the earth but seems small because it is millions of miles away.

The moon orbits around the earth, not around the sun. It is much nearer to the earth than any of the stars, so it looks bigger than they do.

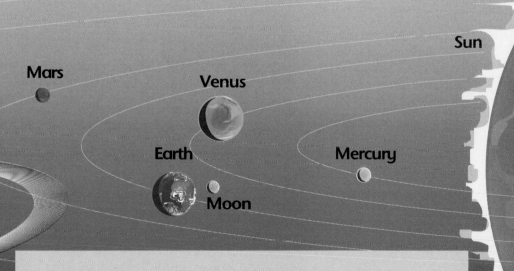

Mars

Venus

Earth

Moon

Mercury

Sun

Mercury, Venus, Earth, and Mars are giant balls of rock. Jupiter, Uranus, Saturn, and Neptune orbit further from the sun and are made mostly of liquids and gases. The furthest known planet is Pluto. It is made of rock and ice.

Water

There is water everywhere on Earth. Much of it is in the oceans and seas, but there is also water on land in rivers, lakes, swamps, and marshes. In cold places, it is frozen as ice and snow. Under the ground, there is water in soil and in the rocks below. In the air, it forms an invisible **gas**.

The water cycle

All water is **recycled**. It travels all the time from the oceans to the land and back again.

❶ When the sun warms the oceans, water **vapor** rises into the air and forms clouds.

❷ Wind blows the clouds over the land, where the water falls again as rain.

❸ Rainwater drains through the ground into streams and rivers.

❹ The rivers carry the water back to the oceans. The cycle begins again.

changing coastline
Pieces of rock and soil are washed into the sea, where they may gradually build up new rocks. The sea pounds against rocky coastlines, slowly wearing the land away.

valleys
Over millions of years, water has shaped the land. Rivers cut into the ground to make **valleys** and **gorges**.

waterfall

river

Rivers, lakes, ponds, marshes, and swamps are full of wildlife. In fast-flowing rivers, only strong swimmers can move against the powerful **current**. Where rivers flow more slowly, reeds and other water plants can grow. Small mammals and birds catch fish and insects to eat.

lakes and marshes
Reeds, grasses, and other water plants grow around lakes and in marshes. They provide food for many water creatures.

water plants

mud flats
Where rivers meet the sea, there are often mud flats. Wading birds dig out shell-fish, snails, and worms to eat.

wading birds

E Aquatic spiders live underwater. They build bell-shaped webs full of air, where they eat their **prey**.

Weather

Sunshine, rain, wind, snow, hail, and fog are all kinds of weather. The weather is the day-to-day change in the **atmosphere**. Movements of hot and cold air, and different amounts of moisture in the air, can make the weather hot and still or cold and stormy.

▲ Hailstones are balls of ice. They can be as small as peas or as big as baseballs.

Climate is the type of weather that is usual in a particular part of the world. **Tropical** places are usually hot and wet. The polar regions are usually cold and windy. About half the people in the world live in countries with **temperate** climates, which are neither very hot nor very cold.

Up in the clouds

Clouds are an important part of the weather, bringing rain, hail, snow, or fog. They are made up of millions of water droplets or ice crystals, so tiny that they can float in the air. Clouds usually form in moist air over the oceans.

Winds blow clouds over the land, where the water they contain falls to the earth as rain.

Sometimes the water in clouds freezes to make tiny ice crystals that fall as snow or hail.

Thunderstorms often happen when warm and moist air meets cold air. Huge storm clouds gather. The raindrops inside them join and grow very big, then fall in a great downpour. There may be flashes of lightning made by giant sparks of **electricity**. They zig-zag between the storm clouds and the ground. Thunder is the shock wave made when air suddenly expands as lightning passes through it.

▲ Thunder and lightning happen together, but we see lightning first because light travels faster than sound.

now picture this

▲ Tornadoes are the strongest storms of all. They swirl into a funnel shape that can spin up to 400 miles per hour.

Very strong winds have been known to pick up tiny frogs and carry them high into the sky. When the wind dropped, the frogs "rained" down.

Whale

Whales are large sea mammals with smooth skins, flippers, and powerful tails, which help them to speed through the water. They are found in all the world's oceans and spend all their time in the water, only coming to the surface to breathe. As they breathe out, they blow a massive cloud of tiny water droplets high above them. Many whales are **endangered** because people have hunted them or they have been killed by **pollution** in the sea.

Did you know?

A whale's nose is called a blowhole and is found on top of its head.

The blue whale is the largest animal in the world. It can grow up to 100 feet long and weigh the same as 25 African elephants.

A whale's heart beats only nine times a minute. A human heart beats arond 65 times a minute.

▲ This humpback whale is guiding her calf to the top of the water to breathe. Humpbacks can go without breathing for over an hour.

Water babies

Whales have their babies, or calves, underwater and usually have only one at a time. Even newborn calves are huge. A blue whale calf is about 23 feet long. Whales take great care of their babies and feed them rich milk. A female whale and her calf may stay together for up to one year.

A song and dance

Whales can talk to each other over long distances. Humpback whales make songs by humming, moaning, grunting, and squeaking. They often leap out of the sea and slap their tails on the water. Every whale's song is different and a single song can last for half an hour.

▶ Dolphins are small, playful whales. They call to each other with clicks and whistles.

▼ A baleen whale

Some whales have teeth. They catch fish and other sea creatures to eat. They are called toothed whales and there are around 65 different kinds, including dolphins. Baleen whales have horny plates called baleen in their mouths instead of teeth. The plates are made of a material similar to human fingernails. They hang like frilly curtains to trap small animals which rush in with each mouthful of water. There are ten kinds of baleen whales.

▶ A toothed whale

Glossary

Adapted Gradually changed to fit in well with the environment. Animals and plants adapt to changes in their environment or do not survive.

Ancestor A member of the same family that lived and died a long time ago.

Atmosphere The layer of air and other **gases** that surrounds the earth.

Breed To raise animals for the purpose of producing other young.

Camouflage The markings on an animal that help it to blend with its surroundings. An animal that is well camouflaged can hide from other animals.

Cattle Cows and bulls that are raised by farmers and ranchers mainly for food such as beef and milk.

Chemical A solid, liquid, or **gas** that acts and reacts in the world.

Comet A body that travels around the sun, leaving a bright trail behind it.

Conifer A tree that has needle-like leaves and produces seeds in cones.

Current Constant strong movement in one direction of the water in a river or sea.

Deciduous A type of tree that loses its leaves in the fall.

Digest To break down food so its **nutrients** and **energy** can be used by different body parts.

Domestic A type of animal that is not wild, but instead kept in the home, or raised on a farm for food or to do work.

Electricity A form of **energy** that can produce heat and light.

Endangered When a type of animal or plant might die out because there are few left in the world or their living space is destroyed.

Energy What makes living things and machines able to move, grow, and do work. Living things get their energy from food.

Equator An imaginary line drawn on maps around the middle of the world, halfway between the North and South Poles.

Fuel A **substance** that gives out **energy** as heat or power when it burns.

Fungus (fungi) A plant that has no leaves, such as a mushroom.

Gas A **substance**, such as air, which is not liquid or solid.

Gorge A deep, narrow passage through land.

Graze To eat grass.

Habitat A place where an animal or plant makes its home.

Invertebrate An animal with no backbone.

Lenses The clear, curved parts in an animal's eye that bring light rays together so that they make a clear picture.

Migrate To move from one place to another, according to the season, to find food or to have babies.

Mineral A natural **substance**, such as iron or salt, that is formed in rocks.

Nutrient The parts of a food that help plants or animals to grow.

Oxygen One of the **gases** in the air. All animals and plants need oxygen to live.

Parasite A small animal or plant that lives on or inside another animal or plant, and feeds off it.

Plain A large, flat area of land with few trees.

Planet A body in space, such as the earth, which moves around the sun or another star.

Pollute To damage the natural world with harmful **substances**.

Predator An animal that hunts and eats other animals.

Prey The creatures that an animal hunts and eats.

Recycle To use something again.

Skeleton The bony frame that protects and holds up the body of an animal.

Star A large ball of burning **gas** in space that, from the earth, looks like a spot of light.

Streamlined Sleekly shaped to move quickly and smoothly.

Substance What something is made from. Solids, liquids, and gases are all substances.

Temperate Where the weather is neither very hot nor very cold.

Temperature How hot or cold something is.

Tropical Found in the hottest parts of the world, near the **Equator.**

Tundra A cold area of land in the north of the world, where there are no trees and the soil is often frozen.

Valley A stretch of land with hills on either side, often with a river running through.

Vapor Tiny drops of water floating in the air, which look like mist.

Vertebrate An animal with a backbone.

Vibration Quick backward and forward shaking movements.

Wingspan The distance from tip to tip of an animal's outstretched wings.

Index